Polar Bears

by Lesley A. DuTemple
photographs by William Muñoz

Lerner Publications Company • Minneapolis, Minnesota

In memory of Flora Overmyer Graham, 1915–1996, with love and appreciation for not only showing me the path, but lighting the way as well.   —LAD

For Chuck Jonkel   —WM

Thanks to our series consultant, Sharyn Fenwick, elementary science/math specialist. Mrs. Fenwick was the winner of the National Science Teachers Association 1991 Distinguished Teaching Award. She also was the recipient of the Presidential Award for Excellence in Math and Science Teaching, representing the state of Minnesota at the elementary level in 1992. And special thanks to our young helper, Jessica Ann Falksen.

Additional photographs are reproduced by permission of: pp. 12, 22, 39, © Harry M. Walker; pp. 13, 16, © Tom Vezo; pp. 17, 20, 21, 24, 25, 28, 29, © 1997 by Kennan Ward; p. 18, Animals Animals / © Doug Allan / Oxford Scientific Films.

Lerner Publications Company, a division of Lerner Publishing Group
241 First Avenue North
Minneapolis, MN 55401 U.S.A.

Website address: www.lernerbooks.com

Library of Congress Cataloging-in-Publication Data

DuTemple, Lesley A.
   Polar bears / by Lesley A. DuTemple ; photographs by
William Muñoz.
      p.   cm. — (Early bird nature books)
   Includes index.
   Summary: Describes the physical characteristics, habitat
behavior, and life cycle of the polar bear.
   ISBN 0-8225-3025-2 (lib. bdg. : alk. paper)
   1. Polar bear—Juvenile literature. [1. Polar bear. 2. bears]
I. Muñoz, William, ill. II. Title. III. Series.
QL737.C27D78 1997
599.786—dc21   97-4131

Manufactured in the United States of America
3 4 5 6 7 8 – JR – 07 06 05 04 03 02

Contents

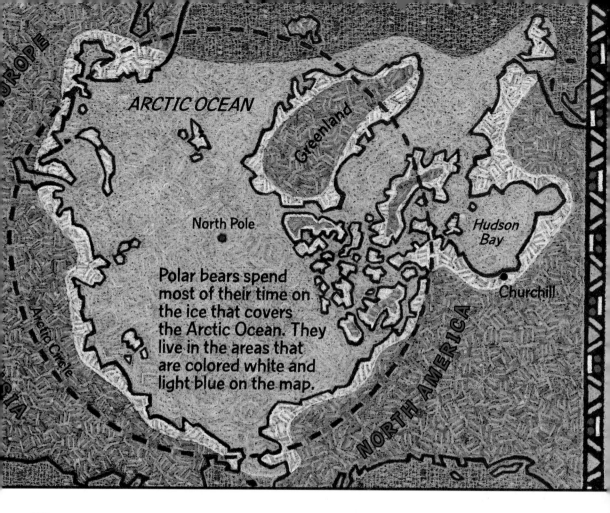

Polar bears spend most of their time on the ice that covers the Arctic Ocean. They live in the areas that are colored white and light blue on the map.

Be a Word Detective

Can you find these words as you read about the polar bear's life? Be a detective and try to figure out what they mean. You can turn to the glossary on page 46 for help.

Arctic	den	migrate
blubber	endangered	nurse
breathing hole	ice floes	predators
carnivores	Inuit	

Chapter 1

Blowing snow almost hides this polar bear. Where do polar bears live?

Bears on Top of the World

High on top of the world, winter lasts for many months. The sun never rises in the sky. All winter, it is dark. The freezing wind howls. Snow swirls over everything. Not many animals could live there, but polar bears do.

Polar bears live in the Arctic. The Arctic is the area that surrounds the North Pole. Part of the Arctic is land, but most of it is ocean. Ice covers the water for much of the year. Even in summer, there is always some ice on the water and snow on the ground.

A polar bear walks across land known as the tundra. There are no trees on the tundra, and the soil under the surface is always frozen.

The polar bear is one of the largest animals in the world. Male polar bears weigh almost 1,400 pounds. That is about as heavy as 25 children. One polar bear could weigh as much as your whole class!

Polar bears are related to grizzly bears and other brown bears. But polar bears are bigger than other bears.

These polar bears are playing. Adult polar bears usually live alone. But sometimes two or three males will eat, play, and travel together.

Polar bears are about 10 feet long. When they stand on all four legs, they are about 4 feet tall. And when they stand on their hind legs, they could look an elephant in the eye.

Chapter 2

Arctic winters are very cold. How do polar bears stay warm?

Black Skin and Clear Fur

Polar bears look white. Their white fur is made of many hairs. But the hairs aren't really white. They are clear and hollow. The hollow hairs trap air. The air in the bear's fur keeps it warm.

A polar bear looks so white that it is hard to see in the snow.

Even though the hairs are clear, the fur looks white because light reflects off the hairs. Some polar bears have tiny plants growing on their fur. The plants make the fur look green!

Arctic winters are icy cold, but polar bears stay warm. On sunny days, the clear fur helps sunlight get to the polar bear's skin. It is like the sun shining through a window onto your skin.

A young polar bear and its mother soak up warmth from the sun.

The fur in a polar bear's ears and on its face is thin, so its black skin shows through.

A polar bear's skin is black. Dark colors take in more heat than light colors do. So a polar bear's black skin heats up more than lighter skin would. The bear's thick, fluffy fur keeps the heat trapped next to its body.

There is a thick layer of blubber, or fat, under a polar bear's skin. The blubber helps polar bears stay warm. So even when they are swimming in icy water, the bears stay warm.

Polar bears have smaller ears than other bears. Bigger ears would stand out and freeze in the cold arctic air.

A polar bear's small ears don't lose as much heat as big ears would.

A polar bear has rough pads and thick fur on the bottom of its paws. The pads and fur help the bear walk on ice without slipping. Everything about a polar bear's body helps it live in the Arctic.

The bottoms of a polar bear's paws are furry.

Chapter 3

Polar bears have long, sharp teeth. What do polar bears eat?

Hunting for Seals

Polar bears are carnivores (KAHR-neh-vorz). They eat meat. Polar bears are also predators (PREH-duh-turz). Predators are animals that hunt and eat other animals.

A polar bear's favorite food is ringed seals. It is hard for a polar bear to catch a seal in the water. Seals swim much faster than polar bears. But seals often rest on ice floes. An ice floe is a large piece of ice floating on the sea. Polar bears hunt for food on ice floes because that is where ringed seals are.

A polar bear waits for a seal to come out of the water.

A ringed seal comes up through a crack in the ice to breathe.

To catch a seal, a polar bear looks for a breathing hole. A breathing hole is a place in the ice where the water is not frozen. This is where swimming seals come to get a breath of air. A polar bear waits next to a breathing hole. When a seal pops up, the bear pounces. It quickly pulls the seal out of the water.

If a polar bear covers its black nose, it is almost invisible in the snow.

Sometimes a polar bear sees a seal sleeping on the ice. The bear crouches down and makes itself flat as a rug. Slowly, it creeps forward. If the seal looks up, the bear stops. It tries to look like part of the snow. It will even cover its black nose with a paw! When the bear gets close to the seal, it pounces.

Other times a bear pretends to be a piece of floating sea ice. It floats quietly in the water. When it gets close to a seal, the bear grabs the seal.

A swimming polar bear is surrounded by sea ice.

A polar bear caught the seal who lived in this den.

In the winter, seals live in small caves called dens. Seals dig their dens in the snow and ice. Polar bears have a good sense of smell. They can smell where seals have their dens. When a polar bear smells a seal's den, it jumps on the den until the roof caves in. Then the polar bear grabs the seal.

Polar bears hunt caribou and other land animals in the summer.

Polar bears hunt all year round. Most animals have an easier time finding food in the summer than in the winter, but not polar bears. In summer, the ice floes break up, and seals are hard to find. Then polar bears hunt other arctic animals, such as musk oxen, caribou, and seabirds. When polar bears cannot find animals, they eat seaweed, mushrooms, or berries. Polar bears become thin in summer. They gain weight during the winter when they can hunt seals again.

Sometimes polar bears eat seaweed.

Chapter 4

A polar bear runs toward the water. How do polar bears usually get into the water?

Swimming in Ice Water

 Polar bears are good swimmers. They spend many hours in the water, moving among the ice floes looking for seals.

Polar bears use their huge front paws to paddle. Their front paws are partly webbed, like the foot of a duck. The webbing helps polar bears swim. They use their back legs to steer. Polar bears do not often jump into the water. Usually, they carefully lower their back feet in first.

The bear splashes into the water.

Chapter 5

A polar bear searches for seals. Why do female polar bears need to eat a lot of food?

Family Life

When a female polar bear knows she is going to be a mother, she spends all summer eating as much as she can. She needs to store up blubber for the winter ahead. She will have to care for her cubs, so she will not be able to hunt for food. The stored blubber will be her food and keep her alive.

A female bear has started to dig her den.

In late October, a female polar bear travels to a favorite place to dig a den. She may return to the place where she was born. Often there are many females in the same area. Their dens are close together, but the bears do not pay any attention to each other. It is like a town where nobody speaks to their neighbors.

The female digs her den in a snowdrift on the side of a hill. Winter snowstorms soon close off the entrance. In December or January, her cubs are born. Female polar bears can have one, two, or three cubs at a time. Most of the time, they have twins.

A two-month-old cub comes out of its den for the first time.

Adult polar bears are huge. But newborn cubs are the size of a guinea pig. They weigh less than 2 pounds.

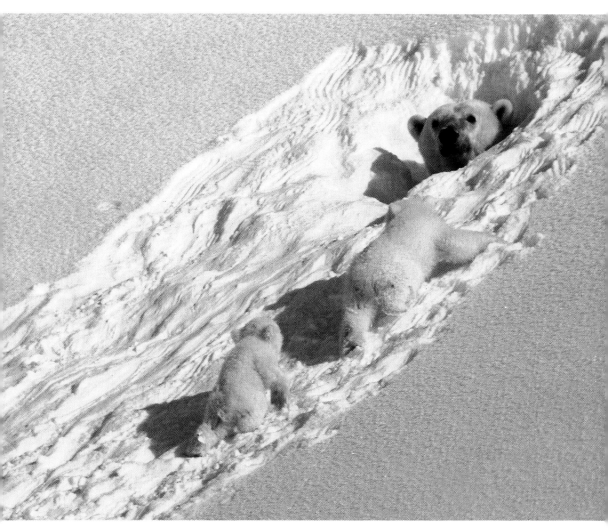

After exploring for a while, two cubs run back to their mother and their den.

Newborn cubs are deaf and blind. They have no hair. They snuggle deep in their mother's thick fur and sleep. When they are awake, they nurse, or drink their mother's milk. After a few weeks, the cubs can see and hear. Soon they start exploring the den and playing with each other. The cubs grow quickly.

Two cubs snuggle with their mother.

*These cubs are
drinking their
mother's milk.*

The family breaks out of their den by about
March. By then, the cubs weigh almost 25
pounds and look like small, fluffy dogs. The
cubs' mother is thin, though. She has not eaten
for four months, and her body has used all the
blubber it stored.

A mother chases another polar bear away from her cubs.

A polar bear mother takes good care of her cubs. She guards them from danger. She teaches them how to swim and how to hunt seals. For two or three years, the cubs stay with their mother. The family might spend the second winter in their old den. But they usually roam in the open.

After three years, the cubs have learned to take care of themselves. They are almost adults. They are nearly as big as their mother. The family breaks up, and each bear heads out on its own.

Three-year-old cubs are almost ready to go off on their own.

Chapter 6

Polar bears travel hundreds of miles each year. When do some bears come to the western shore of Hudson Bay?

Traveling

Polar bears migrate. That means they travel as the seasons change. In the winter, the ice cap around the North Pole gets bigger. Most bears move south in winter as the ice cap grows. Then they move north in the summer as the ice breaks up.

One group of bears comes to the western shore of Hudson Bay every autumn. Hudson Bay is a large body of water in northern Canada. The bears stay on the shore for a few weeks, waiting for the bay to freeze over.

On the shores of Hudson Bay, polar bears wait for the water to freeze.

When the bay freezes, the bears move onto the ice to hunt seals. All winter, they travel southeast, hunting seals. By spring, they reach the southern end of Hudson Bay. Then they turn around. All summer, the bears walk northwest along the shore of Hudson Bay. They hunt land animals and eat seaweed and berries.

A bear looks for seals on the frozen waters of Hudson Bay.

Most people don't want to see a polar bear this close-up!

By autumn, the bears are back on the western shore of the bay, waiting for the ice to freeze.

The town of Churchill, Manitoba, is on the western shore of Hudson Bay, right where polar bears gather in autumn. The bears wander the streets. No people go out at night. During the day, police guard children as they walk to school. On Halloween night, police even help the children trick-or-treat!

A polar bear peers into a tundra buggy.

People from all over the world come to Churchill to see the polar bears close-up. The bears can be very dangerous. But the town of Churchill has learned how to protect both the bears and the people. People can watch the bears from inside tundra buggies. If a bear causes problems, it is kept in a pen. It is let out when the bay freezes.

From the safety of a tundra buggy, people can watch polar bears. And polar bears can watch people!

Chapter 7

Two adult polar bears play together. What is the biggest danger to polar bears?

The Future

 Humans are the biggest danger polar bears face. For many years, the Inuit, the native people of the Arctic, were the only people who hunted polar bears. They hunted them for food and fur. Then airplanes, snowmobiles, and

guns were invented. People came from other places to hunt polar bears for sport. Many polar bears were killed.

Once a polar bear makes it to its fourth birthday, it is safe from almost anything, except orca whales, large walruses, and humans.

Polar bears became endangered. Too many bears were dying. Not enough cubs were being born. To save the polar bears, people agreed to stop hunting polar bears for sport. The Inuit were still allowed to kill polar bears for food.

For every 10 cubs that are born, 7 of them die before their third birthday.

For many years, polar bears have been protected. They are no longer endangered. But scientists still keep track of polar bears. They want to learn more about these great ice bears. With help from people, polar bears will be around for a long time, not just in Churchill, but all over the Arctic.

A polar bear wanders across the frozen tundra of the Arctic in search of food.

On Sharing a Book

As you know, adults greatly influence a child's attitude toward reading. When a child sees you read, or when you share a book with a child, you're sending a message that reading is important. Show the child that reading a book together is important to you. Find a comfortable, quiet place. Turn off the television and limit other distractions such as telephone calls.

Be prepared to start slowly. Take turns reading parts of this book. Stop and talk about what you're reading. Talk about the photographs. You may find that much of the shared time is spent discussing just a few pages. This discussion time is valuable for both of you, so don't move through the book too quickly. If the child begins to lose interest, stop reading. Continue sharing the book at another time. When you do pick up the book again, be sure to revisit the parts you have already read. Most importantly, enjoy the book!

Be a Vocabulary Detective

You will find a word list on page 5. Words selected for this list are important to the understanding of the topic of this book. Encourage the child to be a word detective and search for the words as you read the book together. Talk about what the words mean and how they are used in the sentence. Do any of these words have more than one meaning? You will find these words defined in a glossary on page 46.

What about Questions?

Use questions to make sure the child understands the information in this book. Here are some suggestions:

> What did this paragraph tell us? What does this picture show? What do you think we'll learn about next? Could a polar bear live in your backyard? Why/Why not? How do polar bears keep themselves warm? Where do female polar bears dig their dens? How do polar bears find seals? What do polar bears eat when seals are hard to find? What do they feed their cubs? How is a polar bear family like your family and how is it different? What is your favorite part of the book? Why?

If the child has questions, don't hesitate to respond with questions of your own such as: What do *you* think? Why? What is it that you don't know? If the child can't remember certain facts, turn to the index.

Introducing the Index

The index is an important learning tool. It helps readers get information quickly without searching through the whole book. Turn to the index on page 48. Choose an entry such as *breathing hole* and ask the child to use the index to find out what a breathing hole is and who uses it. Repeat this exercise with as many entries as you like. Ask the child to point out the differences between an index and a glossary. (The index helps readers find information quickly, while the glossary tells readers what words mean.)

Where in the World?

Many plants and animals found in the Early Bird Nature Books series live in parts of the world other than the United States. Encourage the child to find the places mentioned in this book on a world map or globe. Take time to talk about climate, terrain, and how you might live in such places.

All the World in Metric!

Although our monetary system is in metric units (based on multiples of 10), the United States is one of the few countries in the world that does not use the metric system of measurement. Here are some conversion activities you and the child can do using a calculator:

WHEN YOU KNOW:	MULTIPLY BY:	TO FIND:
miles	1.609	kilometers
feet	0.3048	meters
inches	2.54	centimeters
gallons	3.787	liters
tons	0.907	metric tons
pounds	0.454	kilograms

Activities

Make up a story about polar bears. Be sure information from this book is included. Then illustrate the story.

Look at the top of a globe and find the North Pole. Compare the top of the globe to the map on page 5. Do you see where polar bears live?

Pile up your sheets and blankets on your bed. Form a den with them. Imagine you are female polar bear living in a den of snow for four or five months. What does it feel like? If you live in an area where it snows, get permission from a grown-up to dig a den in a pile of snow.

Glossary

Arctic—the area that surrounds the North Pole

blubber—fat

breathing hole—a hole in the ice, where swimming seals come to get a breath of air

carnivores (KAHR-neh-vorz)—animals who eat meat

den—a safe, hidden place. Baby seals and polar bears are born in dens under the snow.

endangered—having only a few of a kind of animal still living

ice floes—large pieces of ice floating on the sea

Inuit (IN-oo-it)—the native people of northern Alaska, Canada, and Greenland

migrate—to travel when the seasons change

nurse—to drink mother's milk

predators (PREH-duh-turz)—animals who hunt and eat other animals

Index

Pages listed in **bold** type refer to photographs.